Introduction to iPad and iPhone

I0004861

The Camera App

© 2018 iTandCoffee

iOS 11 Edition

Special Sales and Supply Queries

For any information about buying this title in bulk quantities, or for supply of this title for educational or fund-raising purposes, contact iTandCoffee on **1300 885 420** or email **enquiry@itandcoffee.com.au.**

iTandCoffee classes and private appointments

For queries about classes and private appointments with iTandCoffee, call **1300 885 420** or email **enquiry@itandcoffee.com.au.**

iTandCoffee operates in and around Glen Iris, Victoria in Australia.

iTandCoffee
Relax, we'll help you get iT

Introducing iTandCoffee ...

iTandCoffee is a Melbourne-based business that was founded in 2012, by IT professional Lynette Coulston.

Lynette and the staff at iTandCoffee have a passion for helping others - especially women of all ages - to enter and navigate the new, and often daunting, world of technology.

At iTandCoffee, **patience is our virtue.**

You'll find a welcoming smile, a relaxed cup of tea or coffee, and a genuine enthusiasm for helping you to gain the confidence to use and enjoy your technology.

With personalised appointments and small, friendly classes – either at our bright, comfortable, cafe-style shop in Glen Iris or at your place - we offer a brand of technology support and education that is so hard to find.

At iTandCoffee, you won't find young 'techies' who speak in a foreign language and move at a pace that leaves you floundering and 'bamboozled'!

Our focus is on helping you to use your technology in a way that enhances your personal and/or professional life – to feel more informed, organised, connected and entertained!

Call on iTandCoffee for help with all sorts of technology – Apple, Windows, iCloud, Evernote, Dropbox, all sorts of other Apps (including Microsoft Office products), getting you set up on the internet, setting up a printer, and so much more.

iTandCoffee
Relax, we'll help you get iT

Here are just some of the topics covered in our regular classes at iTandCoffee:

- Introduction to the iPad and iPhone
- The next step on your iPad and iPhone
- Bring your Busy Life under Control using the iPad and iPhone
- Getting to know your Mac
- Understanding and using iCloud
- An Organised Life with Evernote
- Taking and Managing photos on the iPhone and iPad
- Travel with your iPad, iPhone and other technology.
- Keeping kids safe on the iPad, iPhone and iPod Touch.
- Staying Safe Online

The iTandCoffee website (itandcoffee.com.au) offers a wide variety of resources for those brave enough to venture online to learn more: handy hints for iPad, iPhone and Mac; videos and slideshows of iTandCoffee classes; guides on a range of topics; a blog covering all sorts of topical events.

We also produce a regular Handy Hint newsletter full of information that is of interest to our clients and subscribers.

Hopefully, that gives you a bit of a picture of iTandCoffee and what we are about. Please don't hesitate to iTandCoffee on 1300 885 420 to discuss our services or to make a booking.

We hope you enjoy this guide, and find its contents informative and useful. Please feel free to offer feedback at feedback@itandcoffee.com.au.

Regards,

Lynette Coulston (iTandCoffee Owner)

Introduction to the
iPad & iPhone

The Camera App

TABLE OF CONTENTS

Introduction to the iPad & iPhone

The Camera App

TABLE OF CONTENTS

Introduction

Before we start talking about the app on the iPhone and iPad that allows you to take photos and videos, let's first look at where the <u>actual</u> camera lenses are located on the iPad and iPhone.

It is important to understand this, so that you don't obstruct the lens when taking your photos or videos – and so that you can ensure that the camera lenses are kept as clean as possible! A clean with a glasses cleaning cloth every now and then can really help the quality of your photos!

Did you know that you have two cameras on your iPad and iPhone? There is one on the front, and another on the back.

Finding the cameras on your iPad

Let's look at the iPad first.

The front camera is indicated in the left image below, and the back camera is indicated in the right image below.

Introduction

Finding the cameras on your iPhone

On the iPhone, the front camera is also above the top of the screen, off to the left of the iPhone's microphone.

(The other, smaller circle above the phone's microphone is the accelerometer – which is able to detect when the phone is put up to your ear, turning off the touch screen while you talk.)

The front camera is much harder to detect on the iPhone X – but rest assured, it is there, in the famous (or infamous) 'notch'.

The rear camera on your iPhone looks a bit different to that on your iPad.

On the left below is the rear camera on an iPhone 6S; on the right is that of the iPhone X, providing two camera lenses that allow you to take special photos with an effect called 'depth effect'.

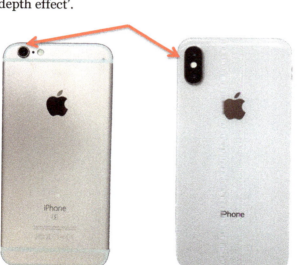

iPhone 7 Plus and 8 Plus also have a 'double lens' similar the iPhone X's. For those models, the camera's have horizontal orientation instead of vertical.

Introduction

How good is your device's camera?

Do you still use a camera, thinking that is capable of taking better photos than your iPhone?

You may be surprised to know how good your iPhone's rear camera is - and the iPad camera on newer iPads is pretty good too!

We talk about cameras and photo quality in terms of 'megapixels'. The higher the number of megapixels, the better the resolution (i.e. quality) of the photo.

The front (i.e. Facetime) camera of your iPad or iPhone will take photos with a lower resolution than the rear camera. The front camera's main use is for 'selfies' and for video chatting using apps like Facetime.

So, use your rear camera to take the majority of your photos.

Here are the ratings for each camera on each iPhone and iPad model, for all devices that run iOS 11.

Back (iSight) Camera

iPad Air, iPad Mini 2, 3	5 megapixels
iPhone 5S, 6, 6 Plus, iPad Air 2, iPad (2017), iPad Mini 4	8 megapixels
iPhone 5SE, 6S, 6S Plus, 7, 8, iPad Pro	12 megapixels
iPhone 7 Plus, 8, 8 Plus, X	12 megapixels (wide-angle and telephoto)

Front (Facetime) Camera

iPhone 5S, 5SE, 6, 6 Plus, 6S, 6S Plus iPad Air, iPad Air 2, iPad Mini 2, 3, 4	1.2 megapixels
iPhone 7, 7 Plus, 8, 8 Plus, X, iPad Pro	7 megapixels

Does your device have a flash?

Your iPhone will include a flash with the back camera, one that can also be used as a torch.

Only the newest iPad Pro's have a flash (those released after 2017) – other iPads do not include this feature.

Exploring the Camera App

On an iPad and iPhone, taking photos and videos on your uses the **Camera App**.

Just touch on the **Camera App** on your Home Screen – and your screen will show whatever your Camera app 'sees'.

What your camera 'sees' will depend on whether the <u>front</u> or <u>back</u> camera is being used.

Make sure you don't have your finger over the lens, or have the cover obscuring the lens.

If the wrong camera is in being used when you start up the Camera App, just tap the 'switch camera' symbol.

On the iPhone, you will find this symbol at bottom right.

On the iPad, it is positioned above the white dot (as indictated here).

Let's now look at all the other symbols you see in this app

Exploring the Camera App

On an iPad (an iPad Pro's options are shown on right), your Camera's options appear on the right-hand side of the screen

On an iPhone (iPhone 6S shown below), the position of the Camera options differs to the iPad – options appear along the top and bottom. There may also be additional options to those that appear on your iPad (depending on the iPhone and iPad model).

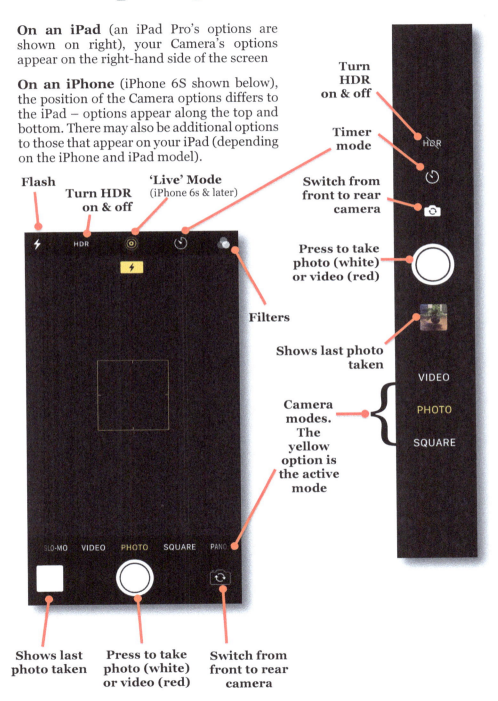

Turn HDR on & off

Timer mode

Switch from front to rear camera

Press to take photo (white) or video (red)

Shows last photo taken

Camera modes. The yellow option is the active mode

Flash

Turn HDR on & off

'Live' Mode (iPhone 6s & later)

Filters

VIDEO

PHOTO

SQUARE

SLO-MO VIDEO PHOTO SQUARE PANO

Shows last photo taken

Press to take photo (white) or video (red)

Switch from front to rear camera

Exploring the Camera App

Most importantly ...

The 'White Dot' symbol allows you to take your photo – you just touch it. But beware if it is instead red, as it means you will take a video!

Before you take your Photo

Before you take your photo (or video), here are a few tips to help you make the most of your Apple Device's cameras – to help you ensure you get the best photo possible

Is the correct camera being used?

As mentioned earlier, if you are seeing your own face instead of the scene that you want to photograph, tap the 'switch camera' option to switch to the back camera (or vice versa).

- On the iPad it is above the white/red dot.

- On the iPhone, it is bottom right.

Set the camera mode to the correct setting

The option that you see in YELLOW is the current shooting mode for your device's camera. Before taking your shot, make sure it is set to the correct mode.

As mentioned earlier, if you see a red dot, you will be taking a video if you touch the dot.

For a standard photo, make sure the camera mode is set to PHOTO.

If another option than **PHOTO** is yellow, (see example of iPad camera modes on the right), just tap the **PHOTO** option if it is visible to select it. (and to turn it yellow).

If the **PHOTO** option is not visible, slide your finger up or down on the iPad until the PHOTO option is selected (i.e. it is yellow).

You can slide anywhere on the screen to change the camera mode options – your finger doesn't have to be over the camera mode options themselves.

On the iPhone (see below), slide your finger from side to side anywhere on the screen to see further options, and to select the PHOTO option.

Before you take your Photo

Get your subject in the picture!

Position your iPhone/iPad so that your subject appears on the screen. Make sure that neither your finger nor the cover is covering the camera lens.

Set the focus and exposure

Your device's camera will automatically try to focus on what seems to be the main object or subject/s of your photos.

A square briefly appears showing where the camera is focused, and the exposure (lighting) is automatically set based on this focal point.

In the above photo, there is a square positioned over the tulips, showing that they are the main focus.

Before you take your Photo

You can change the object/person that is being used to set the focus and exposure by just touching on the applicable object/person on your screen.

This will change the square's position, changing the focus and lighting so that it is optimised for the object/person that you tapped.

In the below example, I tapped on the flowers at top left, so that they were the main focus – the square over the flowers reflects that these flowers will be the focal point when I tap the white dot to take the photo.

Adjust the lighting

As just mentioned, the exposure/lighting is initially set based on the focal object or subject/s that the camera 'sees'.

However, it is sometimes desirable to adjust the lighting – for example, in cases where there may be a bright light behind the subject. In the photo below (taken at the iTandCoffee shop), you will see that, even though the camera has been focused on the face, the light behind has made the subject too dark.

Before you take your Photo

What you may also notice is that there is a **'sun' symbol** on the right of the square that appears to mark the point of focus – i.e. the spot where I tapped.

When this 'sun' symbol is visible, slide your finger up or down anywhere on the screen to turn the brightness up and down.

If you don't see the sun symbol, just tap the screen - on whatever object/subject is the focus. The sun will appear, allowing the brightness to be adjusted.

(Hopefully you will take better photos than mine below, which are just for illustration purposes!)

Automatically detect faces

The newer iPads and iPhones use a feature called 'face detection', meaning they can automatically focus on people, balancing the exposure across up to 10 faces.

You will see a square appear over each of the faces that have been detected by the camera – as shown for the two faces in the image below.

If you wish to focus of the photo to be on something other than these faces, tap on the required object/subject.

Before you take your Photo

A look at Grid Lines and photo composition

Do you see a grid on the screen (as shown in the previous picture)? These criss-crossing lines are there to help you compose your photo.

Apparently, a well-composed photo is supposed to have the main subject off-centre! Did you know this? Something to do with 'the rule of thirds', and the grid lines are to help you with this.

If you prefer, you can choose to turn these grid lines off (or on) – this is done from **Settings**.

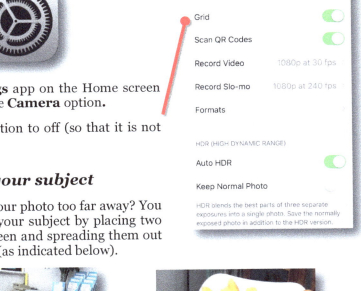

Touch on **Settings** app on the Home screen and go down to the **Camera** option.

Slide the **Grid** option to off (so that it is not green).

Zoom in on your subject

Is the subject of your photo too far away? You can 'zoom in' on your subject by placing two fingers on the screen and spreading them out across the screen (as indicated below).

Before you take your Photo

On the iPad, you will see a bar on the left side (see image below left). On the iPhone*, the bar is at the bottom of the picture frame (see image below right).

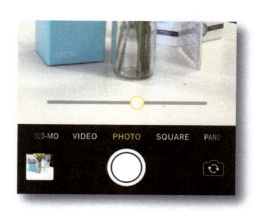

When this bar is visible, you can use your finger to slide the yellow circle up and down on the iPad – or from side to side on the iPhone* - to control your zooming in and out.

* This 'zoom' bar is not shown on the iPhone 7 Plus, 8 Plus and X. Instead, you will see a circle that shows the level of zoom that currently applies, as shown in the example below.

Tap this circle to quickly switch between **1x** zoom and **2x** zoom. Or, use the 'pinch and spread' technique to select a custom zoom setting.

The iPhone 7 Plus, 8 Plus, and X have better 'zoom' capabilities than earlier/smaller iPhones, offering 2 x optical zoom and 10 x digital zoom.

Other iPhones only offer 5 x digital zoom.

So be careful not to 'zoom' too much on iPhones/iPads with 5 x digital zoom, as your image may be less clear. It may be better not to 'zoom', and instead 'crop' your photo later to provide the zoom effect.

Taking a Photo

Tap the dot to take your photo

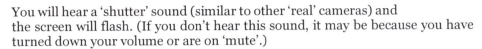

Tap the white button on the screen to take your photo.

You will hear a 'shutter' sound (similar to other 'real' cameras) and the screen will flash. (If you don't hear this sound, it may be because you have turned down your volume or are on 'mute'.)

The photo you just took photo will be saved to your **Camera Roll** (or **All Photos**) in the **Photos** App.

*(For more details about the difference between Camera Roll and All Photos, refer to the iTandCoffee Guide **The Photos App on the iPad and iPhone**.)*

Use the volume button to take your photo

You can also take the photo by using your **Volume Button** on the side of your device. This can make taking a photo feel more like when you use a 'real' camera.

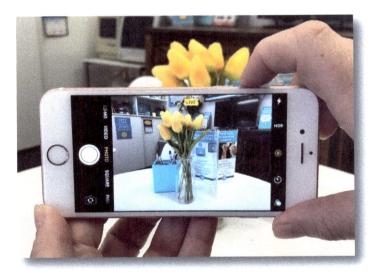

Use your earphones to take the photo

If you have a set of Apple earphones, you can press the middle button of the volume controller/microphone to take the photo.

Taking a Photo

Use your Apple Watch to take your Photo

If you have an Apple Watch, you can take the photo using the Camera app on that device – great for taking a shot that you want to be in yourself!

The Apple Watch app will show what the iPhone camera 'sees' and allows you to tap the dot on the Watch screen to take the photo on your iPhone.

If you keep your finger on the button - Bursts

Just be aware that, if you are a little heavy handed and leave your finger on the white button instead of just tapping it, you will take a quick succession of photos

This is great for when you are trying to get a really nice smile or capture a moving body, but annoying if the extra photos are not required.

If you have an iPhone 5S or newer, or an iPad Air 2/iPad Mini 3 or newer, you will have the more advanced 'Burst' capability that is activated by holding your finger on the white on-screen button.

You will hear a 'rapid-fire' sound, which represents multiple photos being in rapid succession.

Your newer iPhone/iPad is smart enough to then look at that series of photos and choose the best to keep.

You also have the option to view the other photos in the 'burst' and choose to keep some or all of them.

(We cover how to manage your 'Bursts' of photos in the guide **The Photos Guide on the iPad and iPhone**.)

Checking the Photo Just Taken

To check the photo you just took, tap on the small square at the bottom left of your iPhone screen, or below the white/red dot on the iPad.

This little square will show you the last photo that you took.

After tapping this square, you will be taken to the Preview screen to check your photo (or video).

On the right is an example the preview screen on an iPhone, with most options along the bottom. On the iPad, these options appear along the top instead of the bottom.

Swipe from left to right to view the previous photos; right to left to see the next.

If the photo you are previewing is not worth keeping, you can delete it by touching on the trash can.

If you want to send that photo to someone, choose the Share symbol.

If you love the photo, you can mark it as a Favourite (so that you can easily find it later in Photos, in the Favourites album).

Edit You can even edit it straight away by tapping **Edit.**

All Photos Choose **All Photos** (at top right on iPhone) to jump across to the **Photos** app. *(See our separate guide.)*

< To return to the Camera app, select **<** at top left.

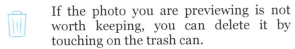

For more information about the first four 'blue' options described above, refer to the iTandCoffee guide **The Photos App on the iPhone and iPad**.

More things to consider before taking the photo

Do you need a Flash?

Is your photo too dark? Are you taking a photo at night?

Only iPhones and iPad Pro's released from 2017 have a flash for use when taking a photo.

To use this, touch on the flash symbol (top left), and select **Auto**, **On** or **Off**.

The **Auto** setting lets your device work out automatically whether or not a flash is required for each photo, based on the ambient lighting.

When **Auto** is chosen, the symbol will show   at top left. When the lighting is such that the flash is going to be used,   will appear at the top middle of the screen to indicate this.

When the flash is **On**, the symbol shown at top left will be

When the flash is **Off**, the symbol shown at top left will be .

Just be aware that some, iPhone cases may interfere with the flash and affect your photos. If you find that your photos taken with the flash suffer 'white-out', try taking off the cover and taking the photo again – you will most likely notice an improvement.

More things to consider before taking the photo

Are you taking a 'Live Photo'?

If your iPhone is a newer model (iPhone 6S or later) you will notice a symbol at the top, one that is not present on older iPhones and iPads - or

This symbol indicates if the next photo you take will be a 'Live' photo – a photo that is actually both a photo, and a very short video.

If the symbol is yellow, then the photo will be a Live photo.

If it is white, the photo will be just a normal photo.

Tap the symbol to turn to 'Live' photo feature on and off.

To view the video associated with 'Live' photo when your preview it (or in the Photos app) just touch and hold (or 'force touch') on the photo until the short video plays.

What is HDR and should it be on or off? **HDR**

Depending on which model of iPad/iPhone you use, you may (or may not) notice the letters **HDR** on your device's screen – at the top of the symbols on the iPad and on the top of the iPhone screen.

HDR stands for **High Dynamic Range**. **HDR**

When **HDR** is active (indicated by the letters HDR showing with a yellow background at top middle of the screen), the camera takes a series of images - each with different exposure (darkest to lightest).

24

More things to consider before taking the photo

It then magically combines the best parts of the three overexposed, underexposed, and balanced photos. This can give beautiful shadowing and highlights.

In the examples shown above, the photo on the left was taken **without HDR**; that on the right was taken **with HDR**.

The **HDR** feature is available all iPads from iPad Mini 3 and iPad Air 2, and on all iPhones from the iPhone 5S.

For all of the HDR-enabled iPads (except for the iPad Pro's released from 2017), you will just have the option to turn **HDR ON** (yellow) or **OFF** (white) by tapping the **HDR** option at top right.

On iPhones from the 5S model onwards, and on iPad Pro's released from 2017, there is an additional option available when you tap HDR at top of the screen – the **AUTO** option.

In **AUTO** mode, your device will automatically determine if **HDR** is needed.

You will see  HDR appear at the top middle of the screen whenever **HDR** is deemed necessary for the photo you are about to take.

More things to consider before taking the photo

There is an important setting that relates to HDR – one that can result in what appear to be duplicate photos.

Because the HDR feature takes more than one photo, there is the option to **Keep Normal Photo** – meaning that you can keep both the 'normal' photo taken without HDR, as well as the one that was put together using HDR.

If you don't want to keep both versions of the same photo, go to **Settings -> Camera**, and turn off the **Keep Normal Photo** option.

On the iPhone 8, 8 Plus and iPhone X, you will also find the **Auto HDR** option – allowing you to choose to permanently turn on the Auto HDR feature.

If this option is turned on, you won't see the HDR option at the top of the Camera App.

Do you want a 'Square' photo?

Is your photo one that you would like to use as a profile shot, or one that you want to use on Instagram?

Your iPhone and iPad allow you to take 'square' photos – photos with matching width and height - instead of the standard "6x4" size of the **PHOTO** option.

Tap **SQUARE** (so that it is yellow), and you will notice the screen shows a square frame instead of rectangular.

You'll notice that, for a **SQUARE** photo, you don't have the option on the iPhone to take a 'Live' photo.

More things to consider before taking the photo

Do you want to apply a Filter? (iPhone Only)

Filters change the 'look' and colouring of your photos, and can be selected before you take your photo

(It should be noted that a Filter can also be applied to the photo after it is taken – so I actually prefer to use that feature of the Photos app instead of applying the Filter in Camera.)

Filters can give some great old-fashioned effects, or even give you a black and white image.

A black and white version of the filter symbol means that no filter is currently selected.

If this symbol is coloured, this means that you have a filter currently selected.

To set (or clear) your filter, tap on the 'bubbles' symbol.

You will see a 'strip' of options along the bottom of the photo frame.

Swipe from right to left to see more 'filter' options.

Tap the required filter. Choose **ORIGINAL** if you don't want a filter.

The picture you then see on the screen reflects the colouring of the filter that you have chosen, and that will be applied when you take the photo.

More things to consider before taking the photo

Do you need to 'lock' the focal point? AE/AF LOCK

You can tell your iPad or iPhone to lock the focus onto a particular position.

This tells your device not to change the focus even if something moves (which might have otherwise caused the device to automatically change its focus).

This is called **AE/AF Lock**, and here's how to activate/deactivate it.

1. Just **Touch and Hold** the screen (on the position where you would like to set the focus until the rectangle pulses, then let go.

2. You will see AE/AF LOCK displayed at the top of the screen. The focus and the exposure remain locked at the position you chose when you touched and held - until you tap the screen again.

3. Tap the screen to release this lock - and you will see AE/AF LOCK disappear from the top of the screen.

More things to consider before taking the photo

Would a Timer help?

Would you rather be IN the photo than behind the camera? Or would you rather take your Selfie without having to reach for the 'dot' to take the photo, and have time to put on your best smile?

Your iPad and iPhone have a **Timer** feature that allows you to set a delay on when your photo is snapped, showing a 'countdown' to help you prepare.

I love this feature – it allows me to set up the iPhone or iPad, by leaning it against something or using a special tripod that I have – and then have time to jump into the scene, so that I am included in the picture.

You can choose between a 3-second and 10-second timer. Here's how

- Tap on the stopwatch symbol at the top of the iPhone screen, or on the right on the iPad.

- You will see the option of **3s** or **10s** - tap the delay period you prefer. The chosen delay will show in yellow.

- Press the white circle to start the timer (as if you are taking the photo now).

- Jump into positon and get your smile on!

- If you are using the 'front' camera to take the photo, you will see a countdown on the screen. If you are using the back camera on an iPhone, the flash will flash to reflect the seconds of the countdown.

- At the end of the countdown, your device's camera will take a 'Burst' of 10 photos and will select the 'best' photo from this burst. (If your device not capable of taking Bursts, it will just take a single photo.)

Remember to go back and turn your timer off when you have finished – otherwise, the next photo you take will use that same timer, which can be annoying.

(For more information about managing Bursts, refer to the iTandCoffee guide **The Photos App on the iPad and iPhone**.)

More things to consider before taking the photo

Do you want the photo's location recorded?

The Camera app on your iPad and iPhone is capable of recording the location at which the photo was taken, so that you can use amazing features of the Photos app to view your photos on a map and to see details of where each individual photo was taken.

While this is a great feature when you are on holidays, it may not be so desirable to have this feature turned on when you are using your camera day-to-day.

You may also consider turning off this feature if the device belongs to a child.

The location-tracking feature of your iPad and iPhone is controlled by something called **Location Services**, which can be found in your **Privacy** settings. This is the area where you determine what apps are allowed to use and record your location.

Visit **Settings -> Privacy -> Location Services** and tap the **Camera** option.

From this option, you can choose to enable or disable location tracking and recording by the Camera app.

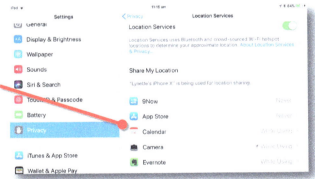

If you choose **While Using App**, locations will be recorded against new photos – but past photos will not be changed.

If you choose **Never**, locations will remain against any photos that were taken while the setting were on, but future photos will not have location recorded against them.

Some special types of photos

Discovering Panoramic Photos

Have you discovered Panoramic Photos on your iPhone and later model iPads?

This is a fantastic way to capture beautiful panoramas and scenic views – or photos of a large group of people.

Slide across to the **PANO** camera mode. (If you don't have this option, then your device does not support panoramic photos).

Here are the step by step instructions for taking a panoramic photo ...

1. Hold your phone in 'portrait' mode (i.e. vertical, not horizontal). You will see a yellow line across the middle with an arrow on the left.

2. Position the phone so that the left-most part of your proposed photo is in view.

3. Touch on the white dot to start recording your panoramic photo – the dot will change a square, to show recording is in progress.

4. Move your phone in a slow, steady motion in the direction of the arrow. I find it helps to tuck my arms in tight and slowly move my body, which helps keep the camera steady and moving in a straight line.

Some special types of photos

5. Make sure the arrow stays centered on the yellow line.

6. If you begin to move too fast or get too far off-centre, you'll see a message on the screen telling you how to correct it.

7. Make sure you take it very slowly – the slower you move, the better the photo

8. Press the square white button to complete shooting of the photo and see your resulting panoramic photo.

(Note. If you want to track from right-to-left instead of the usual left-to right, tap on the right-hand side of the yellow line – the arrow will move to the right side and change direction.)

You can take up to a 240° photo!

As mentioned earlier, this is great for scenery and photos of a large number of people.

Just tell everyone to stay very still, or you might chop off a head or limb (or give extra limbs!), which, while very funny, might not be what you want.

You don't have to take a full 270° photo – you can press the square button to stop at any point.

Some special types of photos

Discovering Portrait Mode

Portait Mode is a relatively new feature, introduced with the iPhone 7 Plus in 2016, and continued with the iPhone 8 Plus and iPhone X.

Portrait Mode allows you to take photos that look like they have been taken by a professional photographer!

Your Portrait photos have what is called **Depth Effect**, which means that the main subject/object of the photo is in focus and the background is blurred.

Depth Effect on iPhone 7 Plus, 8 Plus

On an iPhone 7 Plus or iPhone 8 Plus, you will see the words **DEPTH EFFECT** appear on the screen, to show that the portrait feature will be applied to the photo that you take.

If you don't see these words, you may need to adjust your distance or the content of the photo.

Once again, tap the white dot to take your photo.

If you are too close to the photo's subject/object, the depth effect won't work – so your device will display the message Move farther away.

Adjust your position and try again.

Portrait Photos – Lighting Effects

If you have the newest of the iPhones, the iPhone X, you will have a new Portrait Mode feature that can be used when taking your Portrait photos.

Different lighting effects can be applied to these photos.

Tap the symbol at the bottom and swipe right and left to choose between the different lighting options – Natural Light, Studio Light, Contour Light, Stage Light, and Stage Light Mono.

Then, tap the white dot to take your photo with this special lighting effect.

Some special types of photos

Below are some examples of these portrait lighting effects – have a play with these to see which gives the best effect for your photo.

Recording a Video

Recording a standard video

To take a video set the camera mode to VIDEO.

For this mode (and for another two modes that we will describe shortly), you will notice that the button/dot turns to red instead of white.

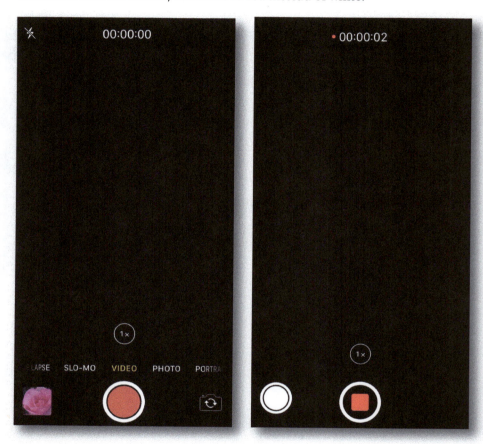

To start recording

Tap the red button icon (or press the volume button) to start recording.

The red button becomes a square, to indicate that recording is in progress.

Recording a Video

To stop recording

Tap the red square (or press the volume button) to stop recording.

Keep an eye on the time

While you are recording, a timer appears at the top of the screen, to allow you to keep track of the length of the recording.

Videos are very big users of your device's storage, so it is important to be aware of this when recording your video – and keep it as short as possible if you are tight on storage space.

Choosing between video quality and size

Before shooting a video, you have the option to select the quality that you would like to apply for the video. The default video quality is **1080p at 30fps**.

This is done from **Settings -> Camera**. Choose the option **Record Video.**

You will see a set of options, which will vary according to the device that you are using. These options allow you to choose the quality for your future videos.

The set of options that I see on my iPhone X are shown on the right.

The size of your video will change dramatically based on the quality that you choose.

The below tables provide details of how much storage is used by a 1-minute video, based on the quality and 'frame rate' you have chosen. The examples shown are from an iPhone 6 Plus and iPhone X.

A minute of video will be approximately:
- 60 MB with 720p HD at 30 fps (space saver)
- 130 MB with 1080p HD at 30 fps (default)
- 175 MB with 1080p HD at 60 fps (smoother)
- 350 MB with 4K (higher resolution)

iPhone 6S

A minute of video will be approximately:
- 40 MB with 720p HD at 30 fps (space saver)
- 60 MB with 1080p HD at 30 fps (default)
- 90 MB with 1080p HD at 60 fps (smoother)
- 135 MB with 4K at 24 fps (film style)
- 170 MB with 4K at 30 fps (higher resolution)
- 400 MB with 4K at 60 fps (higher resolution, smoother)

iPhone X

Recording a Video

As you can see, even just 1 minute of recorded video uses a significat amount of storage. You might also notice that the iPhone X uses significantly less storage for videos when compared to the iPhone 6S. (We'll discuss why a bit later.)

The tables above also show a description for each of the quality levels, giving an indication of why you might choose one over the other, depending on what you are looking to achieve with your video.

Does your video need extra lighting?

Before you start taking your video, you can decide whether or not your video will need to use your Flash for extra lighting. As with taking Photos, the symbol for the flash appears at the top left.

To turn the Flash on, follow the instructions described earlier in this guide for using the Flash for a Photo. As with photos, you have the option of setting the Flash to Auto, so that it comes on automatically if lighting is low.

If the flash is off when you start videoing, you can't turn it on in the middle of videoing (and vice-versa) – you must adjust this setting before you start.

Before you take your video

Before you start recording, think about the orientation of your device and whether you want your video to be able to be viewed in Portrait or Landscape orientation.

For videos that you may want to play back on a computer screen or a TV, it is usually best to ensure your device is in Landscape mode (ie on its side).

Making adjustments while you video

While taking your video, you can use many of the same techniques described earlier for photos – i.e. you can

- Zoom in and out using the pinch and spread method (or tapping the 'zoom circle' shown on an iPad X);

- Tap on the screen to focus on a particular area, subject or object;

- Adjust the lighting by sliding the 'sun' symbol up and down (after you have tapped somewhere).

Recording a Video

Take a photo while you video

So often, we video an occasion or event, and find later that we don't have any photos to go with that video.

The great news is that you can take a photo WHILE you are videoing – meaning that you don't need to choose between a video or a photo of, say, someone blowing out some birthday candles!

This is only possible on an iPhone, and is achieved by tapping the white dot that you will see on the screen. In the example on the right, it is bottom left.

Taping this white dot takes a 'freeze frame' of whatever is appearing on the screen at that moment in time.

The photo taken using this method is not of the same quality and aspect ratio as a standard photo, since it is a 'screen shot'.

But it offers a lovely way of having 'the best of both worlds' – a video, and snapshops of the same special moment.

Other Types of Video

Slow Motion video

Another video option is available by selecting the camera mode **SLO-MO**, (available on all iPhones and most iPads running iOS 11, excluding the iPad Mini 2).

This option allows you to record slow motion videos.

As with standard videos, tap the red dot below SLO-MO to start your recording. To stop recording, tap the red square.

Slo-mo videos can be recorded at 120 frames per second, or at 240 frames per second – a lot more frames than a regular video.

When you play back your slow-motion video, it will play at the standard 30 frames per second rate – which gives the slow-motion effect.

Choose the frame rate that should apply to your Slo-mo video from **Settings -> Camera -> Record Slo-mo**.

iPhone 6S

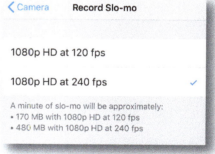
iPhone X

Be careful about using this feature indoors under lights, as you may notice a flickering effect due to the high frame rate of the recording.

As with standard videos, you must be aware of the fact that slo-mo videos take up a large amount of storage space. In fact, they take up around 3 times as much space as the default setting for standard videos.

Other Types of Video

Time Lapse video

The **TIME LAPSE** camera mode offers a stop-motion feature that shoots video at a certain number of frames per second, where this frame rate is on variable scale.

A few good examples of where this is useful is

- For filming the moon rising or sun setting
- For filming storm clouds coming towards you
- For filming something growing
- For filming people coming and going over a period of time.

Before you start your **Time Lapse** video, it is best to have your device resting where it won't be moved – either using a tripod or leaning against something. If you are going to be holding your device, make sure you keep it very still to get the best effect.

As with standard videos, tap the red dot below TIME LAPSE to start your recording. To stop recording, tap the red square.

Compared to slo-mo, where videos are recorded at 120 frames per second, time lapse shoots a maximum of two frames per second, dropping to 1 frame every eight seconds for videos longer than 1 hour and 20 minutes.

Time lapse will alter its rate automatically depending on how long you remain in the recording mode. The effect is to "speed up" the vision taken over a longer period of time.

Your Phone is now a QR Scanner

iOS 11 has delivered a very handy new feature of the Camera App.

Your device's camera is now also a QR code reader. (QR stands for 'Quick Response'.)

You will often see QR codes on products and flyers. They can provide a variety of information about the product, service, etc.

If have a QR code that you would like to scan, hold your camera up so that it 'sees' this QR code.

You will see a message appear, allowing you to access whatever the QR represents – perhaps to jump to a web page, or to call a phone number.

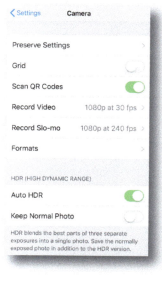

Try it out on the QR code shown below.

Open your Camera app and point the camera at the square shown.

You will see the below message pop up on the top of the screen. In this case, the QR Code represents a link to an iTandCoffee web page.

Tap the message to go to that iTandCoffee web page. Easy!

More Camera Settings

We have already covered several of the settings for your Camera app while describing this app's great features.

There are a few other settings that we have not covered earlier – so here is a description of these.

- **Preserve Settings** offers the ability to preserve certain of your camera's settings, so they do not change each time you come into the app. Below are the three types of setting that can be preserved

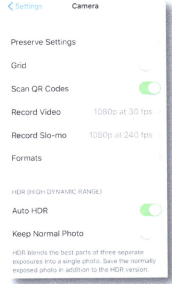

- **Formats:** With the release of iOS 11, some of the newer phones are capable of using a different format for storing images and videos.

  The new HEIF/HEVC format uses less storage than the standard JPEG, which is a bonus!

  Select **High Efficiency** to elect to use the new formats.

  Just be aware that, if you record your images / videos as HEIF/HEVC, you need to consider whether your other devices are capable of handling this new format.

  In the **Settings** for **Photos**, it is possible to set up your device so that any transfer of photos and videos from the device to a Mac or PC will transfer in a format compatible to that other device.

  This in **Settings -> Photos**, under the **TRANSFER TO MAC OR PC** setting. Choose **Automatic** if you have devices that may not 'like' the new format.

Making sure you capture those quick snaps

Quickly get to Camera from the Lock Screen

Have you ever missed a photo because it took too long to unlock your phone and find the Camera app, then press the button to take the photo?

Well, luckily you can get to your Camera app right from the Lock Screen, so that you don't have to unlock your device first.

Swipe from right to left on your Lock Screen to quickly get to your Camera App.

There is no need to put in your passcode or do your fingerprint first!

(On the iPhone X, you get to the Camera app from the Lock Screen using a camera symbol at bottom right of the Lock Screen. Use Force Touch on this icon to open the Camera app.)

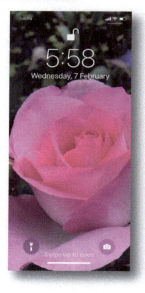

When you have opened the Camera app from the lock screen, you will only be able to preview those photos just taken – not all the other photos that are on the Camera Roll/All Photos. Your device must be unlocked for you to be able to scroll through other photos.

When you combine this quick access feature with using the volume controls to snap the photos, this makes your phone more like an actual camera!

Making sure you capture those quick snaps

Accessing Camera from Control Centre

There is another way that you can quickly find your Camera App – very handy if you are on a different Home Screen, or in the middle of using another app and decide you want to take a photo.

Swipe up from below the bottom of the screen to see your **Control Centre**.

Whether you are on the iPhone or iPad, you will see the Camera App in the **Control Centre**. Tap the camera symbol to go straight to the Camera App.

Control Centre on iPad – combined with   Control Centre on iPhone
Multi-tasking screen

(The **Control Centre** is described in detail in the iTandCoffee guide **A Guided Tour of the iPad and iPhone**.)

Other Guides in the **Introduction to the iPad and iPhone** Series

iTandCoffee has a wide range of guides about the iPad and iPhone, covering topics like

* **A Guided Tour**
* **The Camera App**
* **The Photos App**
* **Typing and Editing**
* **The Mail App**
* **The Calendar App**
* **The Phone App**
* **Shopping the Stores**
* **Discovering iBooks**
* **Getting Connected**
* **And more**

Visit www.itandcoffee.com.au/guides for more information.

www.ingramcontent.com/pod-product-compliance
Lightning Source LLC
Chambersburg PA
CBHW041635050326
40689CB00024B/4969